Hiking With Your Dog: Happy Trails

What You Really Need To Know When Taking Your Dog Hiking Or Backpacking

Hiking With Your Dog: Happy Trails

What You Really Need To Know When Taking Your Dog Hiking Or Backpacking

by Gary Hoffman

ICS BOOKS, Inc.
Merrillville, Indiana

Published by:
ICS BOOKS, Inc
1370 E. 86th Place
Merrillville, IN 46410
800-541-7323

Library of Congress Cataloging-in-Publication Data

Hoffman, Gary (Gary Lee)
    [Happy trails for you and your dog].
    Hiking with our dog : happy trails / by Gary Hoffman.
        p.   cm.
    Originally published: Happy trails for you and your dog. 1st ed.
    [Riverside, CA] : Insight Out Publications, [c1996].
    Includes index.
    ISBN 1-57034-077-3 (pbk. alk. paper)
    1. Hiking with dogs. I. Title.
    [SF427.455.H64   1997]
    636.7'0882--dc21
                                                        97-26303
                                                            CIP

DISCLAIMER

The information in this book has been given based on my experience and research. Taking your dog into the wilderness, or just walking him down the street could have a thousand different scenarios of danger.

Every effort has been made to make this book as complete and accurate as possible. However, there may be mistakes both typographical and in content. Therefore this text should be used as a general guide to hiking and backpacking with your dog, as many unknown medical and legal factors could make huge differences in the decisions each person needs to make based on their conditions and locale.

The purpose of this book is to educate and to entertain. The author and ICS BOOKS, Inc. shall have neither liability nor responsibility to any person or animal with respect to loss or damage caused, or alleged to be caused, directly or indirectly by the information contained in this book.

If you do not wish to be bound by the above, you may return the book to the publisher for a full refund.

AUTHOR'S NOTE

Throughout this book I refer to dogs as "he" or "him" for the sake of easy reading, rather than he/she or it. I have no personal preference when it comes to the gender of dogs and trying to be politically correct makes Fido a dull dog.

– G. H.

DEDICATION

This book is dedicated to my wife, Woodie, whose lovely and caring illustrations appear throughout this book. Without her help, love, and understanding this project would have never seen print.

I would also like to express my gratitude to my cousin, Ginny Greenfield, whose computer skills and talent for layout are surpassed by none.

– G. H.

ACKNOWLEDGEMENTS

I would like to thank some of the people that have helped me through both editions of this book. My sincere apologies if I have forgotten anyone.

My deepest love and gratitude to my wife Woodie, whose wonderful illustrations appear throughout this book, and to my children, Abby and Alex, who I am sure think they never get to see their father anymore. Love to my dogs, Audi and Sadie, who have relentlessly trudged through all kinds of terrain and weather with me, as well as posing for some of my wife's illustrations. And last, but certainly not least, love and kudos to my cousin Ginny Greenfield whose computer skills, mastery of grammar and patience are without rival.

Thanks to David Musikoff of the California Canine Hikers, Linda Von Hanneken of Wolf Packs, Susan Scanlan of Dogs International Magazine, Tom Todd of ICS Books and to the many wonderful people I have met on the internet and in my seminars and travels.

TABLE OF CONTENTS

INTRODUCTION

In the far North, backpacking with dogs has always been common. Here in the United States and Southern Canada there are not many experienced dog-packers to guide people through the particular problems and preparations involved in taking their city dogs into the wilderness with them. Nor has there ever been much in the way of printed material for anyone to use as reference even for a simple hike in the woods. Consequently, campers and backpackers with dogs often end up being a nuisance to themselves as well as others. Untrained, unleashed dogs chasing every bit of wildlife is not what we had in mind when we made the decision to bring our dogs along with us.

Minimum impact camping, proper trail manners and ethics apply to our canine companions as well as ourselves. Dogs, once welcomed everywhere, are now being regulated out of many popular trail areas, with a host of rules and regulations national parks and forests have had to administer due to many occasions of dogs attacking wildlife, campsites, other campers dogs, incessant barking, or just being a general nuisance.

Every pack-dog that ventures out into the wilderness, becomes a representative for all future packers dogs. This is precisely why our dogs must be properly trained and why we must be in control of them at all times.

We bring our dogs with us for the reasons we have them in the first place: Companionship, loyalty, protection, and to share our experiences with an animal in a natural surrounding.

In this book I will try to help you learn the simple techniques to train you and your dog to be prepared and adept at all the skills of dog-packing and hiking, in order to enhance your experience. There are no difficult tricks or elaborate expenses. Just some common sense approaches coupled with time and patience. Patience is a word you will see over and over again as it's importance is paramount to all procedures.

After many years of dog-packing and many miles of trails, I have only on rare occasion seen another dog properly under control. I have had on a multitude of occasions people tell me what a pleasure it was to share camp with such a well trained dog as my flat-coated retriever, Audi. I have always believed in having a dog trained well, if even for my own peace of mind, and I saw no reason not to prepare Audi for the trail in the same fashion I prepared myself.

With that in mind I started documenting the experiences that went into the initial training of Audi when we started packing together. Along with the help of some dedicated dog lovers and the patience of my family, I have put this book together for those of you who have been "hounding" me to write a book on the subject. Soon, I hope that you will be able to experience the joy of sharing a beautiful vista or just collapse with the delightful exhaustion of sharing a full days hike with your dog.

Thoreau said, "He who walks alone, waits for no-one." For those of us who walk with our dogs, we never wait for anyone either, and we don't have to hike alone.

— *Gary Hoffman*

CHAPTER I
Selecting A Dog

People often want to know what kind of a dog is best suited for backpacking. Or simply, will their dog be alright for backpacking?

Essentially any dog can be your hiking buddy. There are too many types of dogs to list all dogs that are suitable for backpacking. Obviously tiny little dogs are not well suited for carrying anything, and some of the short-haired dogs will need more protection than other types of dogs, but there really isn't a dog you couldn't bring along with the right preparation. It is important to keep in mind that breeds with short muzzles such as Bull Mastiffs and Rottweilers have chronic breathing problems. And breeds with extremely heavy bone structure such as the Great Pyrenees and St. Bernard have low energy and less endurance. Ultimately you will need to be the judge of whether or not your dog will make a good backpacker.

Given that the average well trained and conditioned dog can carry approximately up to one third of its weight, in many respects the bigger the better when it comes to carrying ability. Dogs may eat proportionately to their weight, but the bigger dog can bring his food plus carry many other things, perhaps unburdening your load, or giving you the ability to bring things with you that you never would have considered, such as movie or photo equipment, a bigger tent, or better food.

Of course you need to remember that you should be carrying the sensitive equipment and not your dog. And it isn't fair to burden your dog to the max just because he can handle it.

The book *The Right Dog For You*, by Daniel F. Tortora is extremely helpful in selecting a dog. Or go to canine performance events such as herding or hunting trials, agility and obedience competitions and observe dogs and talk to their owners. People are pretty straight forward about the good and bad points of their breed, and most of them are not breeders, so they will not be partisan toward a specific type of dog.

The best dog to bring along is *your* dog, because he wants to be with you and given the right preparation and training he can make your trip more enjoyable. Of course if you don't yet have a dog, and you are planning on making a back-packing pal out of which ever dog you choose, then it would be best to look for a larger dog with the type of personality you like best in a pet. He will of course be more than a hiker, he will be your dog for the rest of the days of the year as well, and it is important that he fit into your daily lifestyle and have a suitable personality for all the types of things you like to do.

My dogs have always been pound puppies, and I have not been disappointed. Be aware that some of these dogs have had very traumatic starts to life and may have a few problems you need to work through or at least be patient enough to overcome until you are trusted. You are saving a dogs life by taking a pound puppy and my dogs seem to understand that, and have been wonderful companions. Older dogs from the pound can be great dogs as well. Most often they are there because the owner was forced to get rid of them because of living arrangements, or a death in a family. The book *Second-Hand Dog,* by Carol Lea Benjamin is a wonderful source of information written with obvious love and understanding. Spend some time researching what type of dog you like, not just because they look great or act a certain way on television. Decide whether or not you can put up with all the problems and work of having a puppy versus getting a dog six or nine months old and make the best choice based on your family situation. Then when you go to the pound or to answer an ad in the paper, take some time with each dog and try to determine what type of personality it has or what type of personality its parents have and make your decision.

My first hiking dog was my flat-coated retriever I named Audi, short for audio (My son is deaf and I taught my dog many commands in sign language.) My current hiking buddy dog is a sheltie-shepherd mix named Sadie. No reason. She just looked like a Sadie dog to me. She is a little on the smaller side, but collie-shepherd dogs are notorious for good personalities and she has turned out to be a very happy companion. Very different than a retriever, Shelties need a lot of attention and exercise and have a much more effervescent personality. More than a lot of people expect or can tolerate. I knew that, but I thought the change would be good for my aging retriever and that she would have enough energy for my kids as well. And I believe that it has been both.

After three operations on my back, and the onset of middle age, I have decided that my next dog will be one of the large variety. I have always had an agreement with my dogs; they carry their stuff and I carry mine, and that is the way it has been. But now, in order for me to bring along all the goodies I have been accustomed to having on my back-packs I am beginning to need a little bit of help.

I have always liked the Alaskan Malamute and the Siberian Husky as a breed, as they are well adept as hiking dogs, able to carry a great deal more weight than what is necessary just for them. Faring well in colder weather and in the mountains where I do most of my hiking, a Malamute or Husky will be right at home. They also have a fairly relaxed personality to fit my fairly stressed life but there are great differences between the two and it will be important to know what they are so that there will be no surprises.

So you see, I am making my selection based on the type of dog I need, and how he will fit into the particular style of living and hiking that I do.

No dog is perfectly suited for everything, and selection is a very personal matter. It's most important to enjoy your dog and be patient in your training and expectations. Like any partnership it takes time, effort, and commitment to make it work.

CHAPTER II
Travel

Breaking your dog into traveling is essential for a successful outing. Dogs can be great travelers as they are always eager to go with you when their experiences have been good ones.

Of course it is best to break your dog into traveling at a young age, but these travel tips can apply to any dog. The exceptions would be if your pet is recovering from an illness, if it is pregnant, or if it is very old.

First of all it is important to have the proper safety precautions before traveling anywhere. Too many pets have been thrown out of the back of pick-up trucks, or end up flying through windows. Your dog is an important part of your family and it is your responsibility to protect it.

There are a variety of belting devices on the market today to protect your pet, and many states have passed laws in order to protect dogs that ride in the back of pick-up trucks. If your dog is riding in the car with you, a simple doggie attachment  to the seatbelts will hold your pet in case of emergencies. If you have a wagon, then a barricade of sorts will do the trick, or some dogs prefer to be kennelled for feeling of security.

Open pick-up trucks have been the greatest danger. There are several harness attachments on the market today, and anyone you can make work will be fine, but please don't forget that your dog is still exposed to constant sun, freezing wind, rain or other conditions. A carpet or a mat in the back will improve traction as well as protect his pads from hot or freezing metal. Perhaps that camper shell you have been thinking about would be a good idea.

Before taking off, make sure you dog hasn't eaten in the last few hours, or has had anything to drink in the last hour. Bring along his favorite toy or blanket and start out with a very short trip. Perhaps five to ten minutes. Either make it a short pleasant ride and then come home, or go somewhere fun for a while and then back home again. Too often the only time he goes for a ride is to the Vet. When you get back be sure and praise him for being such a good dog. The idea is to get him to understand that traveling is fun.

Slowly increase the amount of time you are gone each time, and don't hesitate to bring the kids along as well. Make sure your dog knows that he should be either sitting or lying quietly. Having your dogs head out the window is not a good idea. Often times grit will get in his eyes or nose, or the wind will cause inflammation of the ears or throat. Also if you do need to make a quick stop, this would not be a safe place for your dogs head to be.

After you have worked your way up to longer trips,

it's best to stop every two hours and give your dog a chance to have a drink, and walk around a bit and relieve itself. Bring a bowl for water, and bring his leash. Too often dogs dash out when stopped by the highway to take a break. Sometimes they are spooked by the rushing cars going by, or just excited to be getting out of the car. Be sure and put the leash on them before letting them out of the car.

If it is particularly hot, offer your dog ice cubes, or ice shavings. And if you need to stop and leave your dog in the car on a warm day, make sure there is plenty of ventilation, and park in the shade. Leaving your dog in the car on a hot day, even for a minute or two can be dangerous. Every year we hear stories of people who have done this to their dogs. Plan ahead as to where you intend to go, and where you will be able to stop along the way.

Other things to consider when traveling are making sure your dog has an ID tag, or better yet I suggest tattooing an ID number on the dogs ear or flank and registering the number with the National Dog Registry. Tags can get lost, or thrown away. Bring along any necessary documents, such as a health certificate, or proof of vaccination. A picture is very helpful in finding your dog in case he gets lost.

It is always best to call ahead when traveling to state parks or motels and hotels. Several national chains do accept dogs, but many do not and rooms are sparse and have many restrictions. Check for 800 numbers and call first. Regulations change quickly. See the back of this book, "Names and Numbers to Know" for information on finding motels that take pets. With that in mind, let's begin training.

Chapter III
Basic Training

Just like a child, patience and praise go a long way with dogs. Most dogs are capable of learning far more than we ever try to teach them.

There are many approaches to training a dog properly and there are probably even more to confuse them. Consistency is the key to avoiding confusion.

There are several good books a on basic training for dogs. A few that I recommend are 21 *Days to a trained Dog* by Dick Maller

and Jeffery Feinman. *The Natural Way to Train Your Dog*, by Carol Lea Benjamin. *Communicating With Your Dog* by Ted Baer, and *How To Be Your Dogs Best Friend*, by the Monks of New Skeete. The philosophies and expectations are very different from each other in order to give a fairly well-rounded approach as to how you may be comfortable teaching your dog.

It is essential that your dog be well trained in basic obedience before beginning any actual pack work. The most important command would be to have your dog come when called no matter what activity in which he is involved. For obvious safety reasons this is a critical command that I suggest you work out first, under controlled circumstances and repeat on a fairly regular basis on the trail or wherever you may be together.

I am a strong advocate of hand signals used in conjunction with verbal commands. Often times hand signals prove to be more effective than their verbal counterparts since there can be many situations where the background noise is too loud or you simply do not want to break the silence or disturb the wildlife you may be observing. I have recently read of a deaf Dalmatian that learned numerous signs in American Sign Language, (ASL) which is far more complicated than basic hand commands for dogs. It is estimated that thirty percent of Dalmatians are born deaf, and these dogs learn the hand commands without any vocal prompt. Most dogs are very aware visually, and hand signals used separately or in conjunction with verbal commands will aid in your dogs understanding of what is required of him. This prompts me to point out that it is not necessary to shout out commands. As a matter of fact, dogs come to expect serious commands to be shouted when that is the only way they are given. Any voice, even a whisper will do as long as it is heard. On the other side of the coin, I have found it to be very useful to develop a good whistle, and utilize it when calling your dogs to come to you. They learn to recognize your whistle, and should you be in a situation where your dog has wandered, or can not see or hear you easily, a piercing whistle will grab your dogs attention. Make sure you have praised him for responding and returning to you when you have called. Of course if he was leashed all the time you would never run into this problem.

It can be quite helpful to incorporate different environments in your training. Just because you are training your dog for the trail doesn't mean that you may not have to cross some roads and towns as many trails will do. Getting used to traffic early on will help avoid any possibility of panic or surprise at a dangerous time.

The more situations your dog is exposed to, the less likely the unexpected will scare him. Let your dog get used to other people. Let them pet him. Allow your dog to familiarize itself to other animals such as horses, cattle, or other dogs and cats. All these things are likely encounters on trails. Exposure to other animals early in training will give your dog an edge on any surprise encounters. He will react as an experienced dog should, as opposed to a young dog either frightened or defensive in the face of every new situation.

A variety of different terrain such as grass, rocks, dirt, hills and streams are beneficial to early training. This helps your dog to develop confidence just as experience helps us overcome any fears or anxieties over new situations. I will discuss some of these situations in more detail in later chapters.

It's alright to begin trail training as young as three to four months, but a puppy's muscular and skeletal systems are still very immature. An empty pack or a towel is alright if he will tolerate it. Absolutely no weight at this young age. The early focus should be on behavior. Do not try to build stamina. Remember, this should be fun for your dog. Keep your work times down to fifteen minutes. Let them play a little and go around smelling everything in their new environment. It is equally important that they develop their sense of smell in all these areas so that they may identify danger as well as what is and isn't familiar to the area.

I find most any dog at any age can learn to be a more disciplined and knowledgeable trail dog if the same basic formula is applied.

Even if your goal is simply to go for a stroll in your neighborhood, a trained dog that understands what is expected of him can turn a potentially dangerous or frustrating walk into a pleasurable event for both of you.

CHAPTER IV
Pack Training

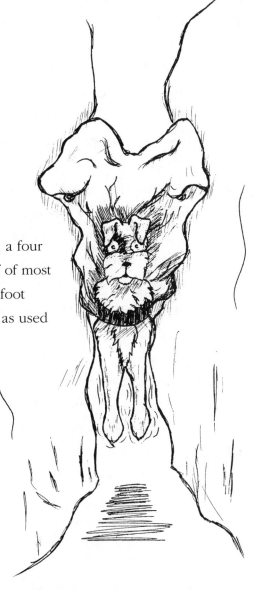

The necessary items to begin pack training are as follows: A properly sized quality pack, a four to six foot pole or staff of most any kind, a four to six foot lead, a carabiner, such as used in rock climbing, and I prefer to use an adjustable semi-slip collar. I will go into more detail on these items as we get further along.

Most packs only come in small medium and large. A good source of packs is Wolf Pack Dog Packs, located in Ashland, Oregon. They have quality packs in all sizes from tiny to extra-large. They also carry the semi-slip collar that seems hard to find at the local dog stores. A proper fit is critical, and Wolf Packs will give you dimensions and selection to fit any dog. Their address and phone number will be found in the back of the book.

For some people color is important. Having a matching collar and pack is fine, but in some instances color can have a purpose. Having a red pack will make your dog visible anywhere, in snow or a forest and he will be easily located by you. Perhaps you have a very well trained dog and while you are out you want to blend in with nature more, observe wildlife. You could select any subdued color or even camouflage. Hunter orange would be a good idea in hunting season. Pretty much the same reasons we select a backpack for ourselves, but there usually aren't many colors to select from in backpacks. In any case, think about the type of hiking you do, look at the selection available and try to make the most sensible decision.

Fit the pack to your dog at home somewhere where there are no distractions. Hopefully by now your dog is standing on command. I feel it is better to start your adjustments at the dogs head as he will be more comfortable seeing you and having you praise him from there.

Whether you are using a one or a two piece pack, placement is very important. The weight should ride over the shoulders, and not down on his back. If you are using a two piece pack, fit the pad to the dog first and then put the loaded pack on him. If you have a one piece pack, it too should be loaded before placement, unless of course it is just a training exercise with an empty pack.

The panniers should hang to about the bottom of the dogs chest, while making sure that the yoke is wide enough for your dogs back. Most packs have a place to attach the leash to, but I think that keeping the leash attached to his collar is best, not only because the semi-slip collar works so well, but pulling on the pack is not a good idea, and when it comes time to take the pack off, he will still have his leash attached to his collar for control.

When filling your pack for an actual trip, it is important to stuff it in proper fashion. Keep the soft stuff on the inside, towards the dog, put the heavier things on the bottom and keep in mind that the front of the pack takes quite a beating. Above all keep the weight from side to side even. Obviously if there is something that you think you may be taking out often, this should go nearer the top, but try not to jeopardize the comfort factor. It adds up after time.

Now, grab the pack and a few treats, hop in the car (belt yourselves in) and find a nice quiet spot with no other people or distractions.

It is best to start with an empty pack on dogs under eight or nine months old. Bones and cartilage are not mature until about twelve to fifteen months,and some breeds such as Rottweilers and Shepards and Belgians are not mature till they are two and a half years old. Allow plenty of time for training before loading a dog down with any extra weight. Put some sweaters or something bulky and light in the pack to simulate the actual increase in width he will need to experience. Build up weight slowly and slowly increase distances.

Next, attach the lead to his collar and clip the carabiner to the left side of your pack or waist belt and have him sit slightly behind you while you move slightly to the right. The use of a carabiner to attach to you is not only for its strength, but for its easy and quick removal.

Placement of the dog behind you and slightly to the left is not exactly the same as obedience school, but this does not seem to cause a conflict with obedience training as dogs will sense the different situation and will eventually know their place with pack on, or when the lead is in place. Placement is important since trails are often narrow and the hiker should be the first to encounter anyone and anything.

Now, with your dog in a sit position, you are ready to start. Give the command to come, and the hiker and the dog move forward. If he tries to dart out ahead of you, simply put the pole out in front of him and say no. Keeping slightly to the right while your dog is clipped on the left allows you to keep an eye on him easier and to maintain the security of walking in an altered heel position for the trail. Maintain training for no more than thirty minutes. Some dogs catch on immediately and some take a while. Be patient, and be consistent with your commands. Keep the lessons short until he has mastered his task and understands his place. Once mastered, you may increase hikes to about an hour. Remember to try and end up on a good note. It is very important that he thinks that hiking with you is an enjoyable outing, and not boot camp!

It is also very important, to teach your dog how to react when encountering other hikers on the trail. Making sure that he is still in the proper position behind you, you may either choose to continue hiking if the trail is wide enough, or have him come completely to the heel position. Many dogs feel more secure by your side. If the other hikers show interest in petting your dog, give him the OK or release command, and let him approach the people, but never let him charge forward to greet other hikers.

My fear is when we approach other dogs. Rarely are they ever under control. It is important to let your dog go slightly ahead in these instances. Not only is it natural to dogs, but if he is forced to stay behind it signals weakness to the other dog. Dog fights are uncommon in the wilderness, but if a fight does occur, in most instances dogs are fighting not for territory, but for dominance. Of course there are exceptions.

Pit Bulls will often fight to the death as the result of cruel training, or an abandoned dog may be sick or frightened. The wilderness, the park or the outdoors in general is no-ones territory, so consequently there are much less instances of dogfights.

Should a real fight occur, the recommended procedure is to determine which dog is losing, and yank its back legs out from under it. Even if it is your dog! This will cause him to go down and the other will feel that he has won dominance. This is not always an easy thing to do and must be done with a great deal of assertiveness or you will only cause the losing dog to slip and panic which will increase its chances of being bitten. Pulling off the stronger dog will increase both of your chances of being bitten, plus it will give the other dog a chance to recover and possibly prolong the fight.

Check your local laws as to the use of mace or pepper sprays. These are a great defense against a loose aggressive dog or animal, without having to actually harm them.

You will find a great deal of controversy on how to handle fights, or whether or not you should at all, since most fights are not as serious as they may sound. The majority of times when two dogs meet on neutral ground, they simply go through their sniffing and identifying rituals and then with a little encouragement are once again on their merry way.

When we hike we share the trail with many others. When meeting up with a horse or a team of horses or mules or most anything else, you and your dog should give up the right of way. The lead line should be on your dog and in your grip, and you should pull yourselves well off the trail until they have passed.

Encounters with wild animals are rare. It is essential to remember that this is their home and territory and they are not out looking for you or your dog. Every day is survival to a wild animal and if your dog is properly trained and secured there is little you will have to worry about. Hopefully your dog has had his rabies vaccination and is up to date on all other necessary shots in your area. Contact with other animals that produce cuts or scratches will have to be assumed as being exposed to rabies, and unless your dog has been vaccinated you will need to bring him to a vet immediately. A booster shot is recommended if he has had shots and gets cut.

I do feel that it is important that these early outings be a one-on-one relationship. A second person often interrupts the rapport. Outings with other hikers and their dogs can be a lot of fun, and generally does no harm, but it is not a good setting for training purposes. A veteran dog can adapt to all kinds of changes, but a novice dog will be distracted by random play of other dogs and the chatter of other people, although dogs do learn from other dogs.

Don't expect your dog to overcome all obstacles at first. All trips are valuable lessons and a storehouse of information. The experience is too important to be rushed. Patience. Everything your dog does with the pack on is a new experience and in every hike he is learning his place behind or next to the trainer. He needs to watch and pay attention. He will eventually find your pace. and soon there will be no more stepping on heels, or crashing into you when you suddenly stop. Attention should be mutual here. The hiker must learn to listen to the dogs breathing and footsteps as he hikes behind you. If your dog should stop, so should you. Whatever the reason. Often it is just to relieve himself, or perhaps he has picked up on a smell that has aroused his attention. It is important that your dog know you respect his needs and his curiosity. This is the making of a partnership. We haven't gone through all this just to bring our dogs with us to command. He is along to enhance our experience as well as to share it. Once he gets comfortable and becomes a good trail dog, there is much that can be learned from observing him. My dogs become my ears and my nose, and often my eyes. Always on guard duty, at night I feel like I can relax more than I used to when I hiked without dogs. Their incredible sense of smell and awareness often alerts us to danger or often times other birds or animals of which we may not have been aware. When we learn to pool our abilities, the making of a team and not master and dog give us a greater sense of sharing the wilderness for our mutual benefit.

CHAPTER V
Equipment

People do not seem to hesitate to bring a slew of goodies to make themselves more comfortable, such as sleeping bags, wind and rain gear, extra socks and clothes, but rarely do they do the same to make their beloved pet more comfortable.

Dogs are not wild animals anymore, as they have become accustomed, as we have, to a certain degree of comfort. Dog booties, a parka, rain gear, and a tarp for cover or to lay on is just as necessary for your dog as it would be for you. It's just that he doesn't complain. Refer to the list of necessary items to

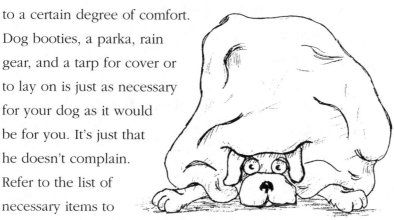

bring as items that are routinely part of your dogs pack the same as the items in your pack are part of your routine. Keep them updated on a regular basis. Be especially aware of dates on medical supplies and keep a check list.

Equipment List

These items should be considered a must for a trip of any duration. Don't feel that this is all there is. You will eventually devise a list of your own suited to you and your dogs particular needs and locale.

Your basics:

- ☐ Sighting compass
- ☐ Map of the area
- ☐ Bandanna
- ☐ First aid kit* (see first aid kit items below)
- ☐ Emergency blanket
- ☐ Knife (I now bring a multipurpose tool such as a Leatherman)
- ☐ Insect repellent
- ☐ Emergency food
- ☐ Flashlight with extra batteries and bulb
- ☐ Sunglasses
- ☐ Flint
- ☐ Compass
- ☐ Metal cup

☐ Matches in water-tight case

☐ Water filter or purification tablets

☐ Pen and paper

☐ 100ft. of parachute chord

☐ Whistle

☐ Toilet paper

☐ Soft nylon tarp

☐ First aid book (laminated or in plastic)

(I can carry all these items in a fanny pack. If I need to
take more I go to a day pack.

Clothes:

☐ Hat

☐ Wool socks

☐ Rain poncho

☐ Gloves

☐ Sweater

☐ Waterproof hiking boots

Your first aid kit:

☐ Snake bite kit (Extractor)

☐ Percogesic

☐ Aspirin

☐ Triple antibiotic

☐ Alcohol swabs

☐ Diarrhea medicine

☐ Scissors

☐ Tape 1" X 10 yards

☐ Moleskin or molefoam

☐ Medium butterfly bandages

☐ Elastic bandage 4" X 10 yards

☐ Tweezers

☐ 1" X 3" bandages

☐ New skin or second skin

☐ Sewing kit

☐ Ethilon suture

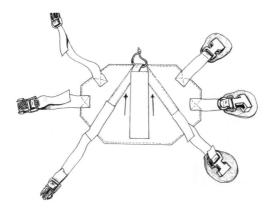

Dogs Basics:

☐ Pack

☐ Extra collar and leash

☐ Collapsible bowl

☐ Food (in baggies)

☐ Booties

☐ Parka

☐ Rain vest

☐ First-aid book (laminated or in plastic)

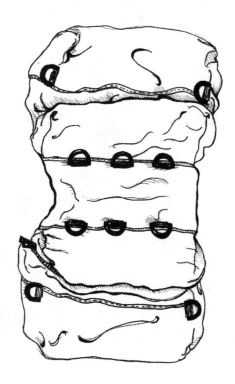

Dog First Aid Kit:

☐ Adhesive tape 1" & 2" rolls

☐ Gauze bandage rolls 1" & 2"

☐ Sterile gauze pads 3" x 3" & 4" x 4"

☐ Scissors

☐ Vet wrap

☐ Mosquito and tick repellent

☐ Safety pins

☐ Hydrogen peroxide*

☐ Anti-bacterial soap

☐ Eyedropper or dose syringe

☐ Boric acid eyewash*

☐ Aspirin* (not a non-aspirin product or ibuprofen)

☐ Razor blade

☐ Snakebite kit

☐ Tweezers

☐ Needle nose pliers (your multipurpose tool)

* These items can be put in small bottles found at backpacking stores. Label them and date them. Keep a checklist in your first-aid kit.

CHAPTER VI

Advanced Training

At this point your dog is able to carry approximately one-third of it's weight for the better part of a day with proper rest stops and nourishment. Now we will go over some of the obstacles you may encounter such as stream crossings, narrow trails, rock scrambling, and drop-offs. If it is possible to arrange some of these obstacles for a day hike, I suggest you do so. If your dog flatly refuses to cross a rapid moving stream, this is the time to find out — not five miles in on the back pack you have planned all year. Having an alternate hike planned nearby would be wise.

Stream Crossings

Assuming your dog has had some simple encounters on your day hikes with slow moving streams he should not be afraid to try a bigger stream. Try and find an easy crossing for your dogs first encounters as this will help him build confidence as more treacherous situations arise.

He should be walked, not dragged into the water, while you are talking calmly to him. He will be looking and listening to you to hear fear or disgust in the manner of your voice or in your actions. If you can not get him to go, try removing his pack. The pack is as you, and by now your dog knows, a disadvantage in more ways than one. First of all it is extra weight, and when it gets wet it gets really heavy. Although the drain holes serve well to empty the pack after it has been submerged they are not necessary in a quality pack. Secondly, the pack greatly increases the surface area the water can push against. If your dog is swept off his feet, the additional weight of the pack can tire him quickly and easily. As a rule of thumb, I suggest when the water in a stream reaches the bottom of the dog-pack, remove it and have your dog cross without it. Have your dog stay, and cross the stream yourself with your pack and his pack, and then come back to negotiate you and your dog. This will also give you an opportunity to negotiate the crossing first for potential hazards, and your dog will see that you have survived the ordeal twice!

I have seen people attempt to carry their dog across streams and rivers. Unless you have a chiwawa, I believe this is very dangerous as the additional weight of the dog makes the hiker top heavy and dealing with a frightened, squirming dog in a potentially dangerous situation will add to your likelihood of disaster. Time to take out your topographic map and look for an area more likely to have a simple crossing or better yet no stream.

The best place to cross a typically free flowing river would be at its widest point as it is most

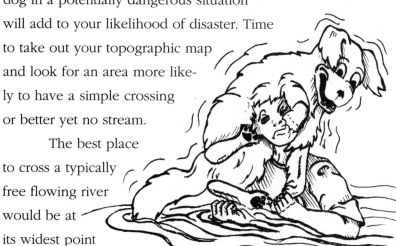

likely to be the shallowest. Make sure there isn't a steep bank on the other side you're headed for. Face slightly upstream for maximum stability and to see debris floating downstream. Keep your feet at shoulder width. If you have your pack on be sure to un-clip the waist belt for easy removal in an emergency. Also, if you are wearing gaiters, take them off. You may want to slip into sneakers and shorts to keep your hiking clothes dry. If you are entering the stream in your boots, loosen the laces slightly in case your foot gets stuck. If you set up a taught line, the rule is never to tie yourself to it. Once in the water, use your staff to probe for holes in the river bed and act as a third leg. Be sure to avoid fast water, and check for root tangles. Speak calmly and let your dog follow you.

It helps to plan your trip well so you have an idea of where and when you might encounter fast water and either have an alternate route or an alternate trip in mind. Spring run-off means fast water in places that may have seemed easily manageable last Fall.

I usually just plain avoid fast water. If the stream is an obvious simple crossing, I unhook the dogs and cross slowly and carefully. If there is any doubt as to the speed of the current or obstacles underneath I will go first with just my pack, un-clipped and then come back for the dogs pack, and then my dog. By then I have truly mastered the stream crossing and there should be no surprises.

The prudent packer will avoid any potential disasters.

Some of my most rewarding trips have been ones that had been re-routed for one reason or another due to my dogs or my own limitations. Have faith in whatever hand nature may play in guiding you along its paths.

Bouldering

Throughout the United States boulder navigation is a situation faced everywhere above timberline, and often along streams and rivers and just about anywhere in the Southwest, or so it seems.

River boulders or boulders found in canyons are often smooth and very slick, especially when wet, and other boulders often times are granite and feel like rough sandpaper on tender pads. You try hiking barefoot! Some people make a preperation of tannic acid from tea to toughen dogs pads, though there are several products on the market that claim to work well.

Most dogs will jump from boulder to boulder with many jumps of two to four feet. Proper navigation here with the dog in mind is critical. We have hands to climb, and hold on, and dogs do not. Choose your routes carefully. I have had to turn back more than once.

The correct procedure for boulder terrain is to remove the lead line, and adjust the pack for boulder travel before beginning. The pack needs to be perfectly balanced. Remove some water from one bottle or add a few small stones to one side to even the pack. Whatever is necessary for a perfect balance. As little as one pound off- balance will tend to sway with each leap throwing your dog off-balance.

After properly balancing the pack, you may want to secure it with the nine foot auxiliary strap if you have one. This is what it was meant for. The strap secures the balanced pack tightly against the dog, decreasing sway and giving him a tighter profile between boulders.

I suggest you practice putting this strap on your dog at home a few times before attempting it on the trail. It's not really difficult, but it can be confusing the first time, and the trail is never the best place to see if you can figure out how it goes. It would be prudent to take the diagram of how the strap goes on and have it laminated and keep it in the dogs pack along with his first aid book.

A common injury when traversing boulder fields, or scree slopes is a lacerated pad. Even though your dog may be quite used to hiking, and have relatively tough pads, sharp stones or granite can still lacerate their pads. If this occurs, it is best to stop and rest. Use direct pressure with a clean dressing to stop the bleeding and put a dog bootie on the injured foot. Check the other pads and if they are beginning to look a little worn, go ahead and put booties on the other feet as well. The vet wrap you brought along will work well to hold the booties up. Remember this is a little bit more awkward for your dog, and he probably won't have the traction he is used to either, so it is necessary to evaluate your situation at that point to decide whether or not you should go on. Sometimes it might be best to head back if you can. This is not something that is going to go away quickly. If your dog begins to limp, you can carry his pack for him by securing it to your pack using the nine foot strap. If he is still limping, stop and

check for any swelling. If there is swelling present, loosen the pressure on the top of the bootie, and go along as easily as you can back to your car.

Drop-Offs

Another potentially dangerous trail condition is a narrow drop-off on either or both sides. Often these trails are found on mountain ridges, or running along rivers. Quite common is bad footing which presents the need to move along steadily and surely. Remove the lead line, turn to your dog and calmly tell him "it's alright" or "OK" or some word you might use to attract his attention to a special situation but not to alarm him. Unclipping the lead line should never be a gesture for your dogs freedom without a release command.

Unclipping the lead should alert your dog to a situation that needs to be navigated carefully. Eventually it will.

Most dogs don't seem to have a problem with trails like these. Their balance and sure-footedness is closer to their nature than ours. They should be used to the pack before they encounter these situations and I again stress an evenly balanced pack is critical. The nine foot strap can be used here as well to secure the pack although it is not absolutely necessary.

CHAPTER VII

Adverse Weather

Snow and Cold

When hiking in snow, the hiking staff works well as a probe to check the snow as to where it will hold weight, and where there is safe footing.

It is necessary to make frequent stops when hiking in heavy snow, to clean ice balls from between the pads of your dogs feet. If left unattended these ice balls can cut deeply and injure the dog.

Dogs have no traction on ice, and have trouble with footing in deep snow. Pay close attention for glazed slopes or any potential area that loss of traction would result in an accident. Often times it is necessary to unclip the lead line to let them navigate through trees, and when there is a hazardous or slippery area it may be best to hold on to their collar for a short distance.

Cross country skiing with some dogs is too fast paced for safe snow travel. But for others it is fun and safe as they trot along in the tracks, even in deep snow.

Although snowshoeing is a good pace and allows for a quiet winter hike, often when snowshoes are necessary the snow may be too deep or soft for your dog. Check it out, plan ahead, and be on the lookout for potentially dangerous snow covered situations.

Long-haired dogs do well in Winter. They seem quite comfortable hiking or rolling in the snow. A short-haired dog is more likely to need a parka and sleep under cover. Your dog may not be used to sleeping outside in cold weather even if he has a very thick coat, remember it takes animals a while to be acclimated to these kind of conditions. My long-haired retriever refuses to sleep in the tent with me regardless of how cold it is outside. If I know I am going to be in very cold weather I'll bring along a ground tarp and put her coat on her before retiring.

Check occasionally for faint blood marks in paw prints. Though the paws may look perfectly normal, the cold brings the warming blood to the surface of the paw. Not to panic though, this is a warning that your dog has extended his system in order to maintain. Resting will help and the symptoms often subside. If the pattern repeats, all activity should be halted.

Animals, just like people, need to become accustomed to their environment. When a dog has not been gradually acclimated to the snow and cold of winter, going out and starting a hike would be quite a shock. Dogs can get used to extreme cold temperatures if they are slowly introduced. The problem is that most of the time we don't have the time or proper conditions to prepare. This is where extra clothes, cover and even doggie sleeping bags allow us to expose our dogs to the elements without fear. Most newer tents have vestibules which offer decent protection without having your dogs walking all over your sleeping bag or tearing holes in the bottom of your tent. I might point out here that it is a good idea to trim your dogs nails a week or two before you hike so that they are of proper length and not tender. Not just for the sake of your tent, but for their feet. If you do keep your dogs in with you, an extra tarp on the floor will keep the floor from being torn.

Heat and Dehydration

Let your dog drink all it wants. Plan your trips where water is available, or carry extra water and offer it often. Keep in mind that all water is considered tainted. Yes even a dog can get Giardia. It is very difficult to teach your dog not to drink out of streams and puddles. All water should be filtered rather than treated with iodine, since a buildup of iodine can be hazardous, although one or two days will

not likely cause any problems. Of course getting your dog to drink iodine treated water may be difficult unless you carry the ingredient that takes the taste away. Boiling, of course is the other option. This is tedious as you need to bring the water to boil for five minutes and then let it cool. Teaching your dog to drink from squirt bottles as you rest along the way, is easier than filling up the collapsible container every time you both need a drink, though either would be fine.

Try to travel in the early morning hours and take many rests. If water is short, it is best not to eat as this requires even more water that is necessary for digestion.

Some people use a little sun block on dogs sensitive noses. I don't know. They lick it off right away, and it can't be good for them internally or externally, but I have friends who swear by it. Everyone seems to think that Avons "Skin So Soft" works well as a bug deterrent. It may help, and I don't think it could hurt. For dogs, mix a capful or two in a quart of warm water and work it into your dogs coat. Put a little bit inside and around their ears as well. Best if you bathed your dog first.

For some reason people think it is easier to adapt to heat than cold. Even if that is the case for you, it may not be for your furry friend. If your dog is panting and heading for the shade all the time, he is trying to tell you it is time to rest. Make sure and check for dehydration. Simply lift the skin above the shoulder blades and drop it. It should drop right back in place if the dog has proper hydration. Try this at home first so you can see how it should be.

If you are going to an unfamiliar area or just off the beaten path, the radio and television weather generally won't cover it. Its best to talk with the National Weather Service office or often times a BLM or park ranger office can help you. Ask about highs and lows and any storm fronts that might be moving toward the area you are planning on hiking.

Mark Twain talking about the weather once said, "There is only one thing cer- tain...there is going to be plen- ty of it."

CHAPTER VIII

Does A Dog Shit in the Woods?

I realize that this is the kind of subject people don't really want to discuss or read about in great detail, but it needs to be dealt with briefly.

Certain parks or places may have their own rules about dog doo, but if you are in doubt as to what to do when there are no hard and fast rules, just put yourself in the place of the next person who comes down the trail and ask yourself if this is what you would want to see. Or step in.

Basically animals will be animals, and the

fact that coyotes and rabbits, and yes even bears do shit in the woods whenever and wherever they feel like, should, with just a few exceptions, hold true for dogs.

One argument is that horses on the trail leave a tremendous mess and no one is making anyone pick that up. But that doesn't make it right. I don't really expect anyone to trail horses and clean up after them, and I generally try not to take a trail where there might be horses. But I still go back to the fact that I wouldn't want to leave anything that I wouldn't want to see myself. If my dog has to leave one on the trail, it is not too difficult to toss it off somewhere else. And around the campsite, not only do I not want to smell it, I do not relish the possibility of stepping in it. It also attracts flies. So generally I bury it the same way I would bury mine. Six inches underground is a depth that is safe to step on and it is in the area of soil that will decompose the quickest.

Since packing it out is not a reality for me, moving it or burying it is not that much trouble. The next time you set up camp and it is clean and free from any evidence that anyone else was ever there you may appreciate it and remember to leave it the same way. Enough said about this. Let us move on.

CHAPTER IX
Extended Trips

Extended trips require more effort and challenge the full potential of a pack dog. Basically you can go for as many days as you and your dog can carry food. Depending on the size of your dog, the difficulty of the trip, and his particular eating habits, it should be fairly easy for you to determine your dogs individual limits. I do suggest having one extra day of food though, just in case. And don't forget to let someone know exactly where you are going and when to expect you back.

On a one or two day hike I usually feed my dogs an extra cup of food at dinnertime. They always get a milkbone in the morning. A dog on a backpack should generally be fed twice a day as well. Food is energy and a light meal or a milk-bone about an hour before hitting the trail is what I usually recommend. Then a normal meal at the end of the day. A heavy meal can cause bloat. Bloat is a condition where the stomach can twist upon itself and become blocked. This is a very serious condition that often leads to death. Be sure to bring his normal food along as change in diet will upset his stomach. If you are running out of his normal diet and need to change, then gradually mix the old with the new and it will be an easier transition for your dog.

On long trips I suggest several extended rest stops during each hiking day where the packs are removed. With the pack on, the dog seems more geared towards the work relationship, but with the pack off, it is more a of a break-time for him.

When you stop, make sure and check for ticks, and check his pads. There are some fairly effective flea and tick collars on the market, but they are not a save-all. As to the pads, if they are looking raw, don't wait until they are sore to put the booties on. It may be a good idea to plan a day at camp if either one of you needs to heal a while.

Clean yourselves up a bit, and relax. Maybe a swim or a siesta in the shade is in order. Days should be planned out where they are not in such a rush. Enjoy wherever you are.

Long trips offer a great deal more time to (forgive the ancient term) get in a groove. As the days go by, your dog will become more comfortable with the agenda of hiking during the day and not coming back to the house at night. It lends itself to a more relaxed and understood daily routine, that seems to be as memorable for your dog as it was for you. A lot can be achieved in the relationship between you and your dog when sharing a long trip. It gives the necessary time and atmosphere that goes with full and exciting days put back to back.

But of course the risks are greater as well, and when planning a long trip, you must be sure that both you and your dog are up to it. Just as you should prepare for any long backpack, with all the proper maps, food, medical items, etc...

Unfortunately, this is often beyond the means of many people and it does not mean that you could not set up a similar situation with a greater degree of comfort. A lot has to do with just getting away for an extended period of time and sharing each day in a more relaxed and beneficial fashion. Too many vacations are planned with getting someone to watch the dog, while we are hustling and bustling through every day only to return needing more rest than when we began.

I suggest rethinking some trips and take the family and the dogs with you and capture some of the times you may easily otherwise pass by.

CHAPTER X
At Camp

When arriving at your campsite, it is important to be aware of your surroundings and to keep track of your dogs whereabouts. With his pack off, he is apt to break some of the rules he adheres to when working. Give your dog his freedom to explore your area, but be sure he is under control.

If this should become a constant problem, then secure him on the long lead. The exploration of a campsite should not be dis- couraged though.

The familiarity will add to the dogs understanding of his environment, and will help him to know what should and shouldn't be.

Protection is a part of a dogs conduct in his new surroundings as they are focused intently on all the sounds and smells. An experienced dog will relax more quickly, being more familiar with what sounds and smells to be concerned with.

I would like to point out that taking a bitch in season should be avoided. Wild canines are attracted by the smell and will often times boldly approach your camp at night. Male dogs from other campsites may also come calling.

I prefer to avoid bear country when back-packing with dogs. Dogs will sometimes provoke an attack on a bear cruising for food. On the other hand, some people I've talked to seem to feel that a couple of veteran dogs can ward off a potential bear attack. Of course prevention such as bear bagging food, and keeping your dogs in control generally avoids any such occurrences, but there is simply not enough known to say what is best. I certainly would not be in Grizzly country without a firearm, and it has been my experience that if my dog is tied at night, that his barking alone seems to scare off bears or any animals who might otherwise be nosing through for food.

As your dog gains more experience he comes to know what is expected of him. It is important that you guide him to realizing these situations as well. For example, a veteran dog will wait to drink water, will not take off after animals and birds, never pushes up against the hiker, realizes potential danger, and warns the hiker. A veteran dog will negotiate difficult terrain, and follow all commands and hand signs. Kind of like a Dog Scout Oath.

While we rest at camp our canine companion feels at home with us wherever we set our tent. There is even more peace and relaxation as our dogs become our ears. We can tune out and listen to the night sounds we love, for he is always on duty to identify an unexpected sound or smell.

As we sleep in our bag under the night sky, deeply entranced in our dreams, our companions are never seemingly so deeply asleep. Always aware, always ready, he will accompany you at any hour, anywhere, ready to fight anything to defend you. No questions asked. There is a kind of telepathy between man and dog. As time goes by, our dogs tune into us. They know our habits and observe our emotions. Through their relentless desire to please, and protect, eventually we reach a harmony. With mutual respect we live together and play together.

Through nature we grow as humans. In our seeming superiority we have a great deal to recapture through an animal, whose willingness, and devotion, is unparalleled in this universe.

CHAPTER XI

First Aid

Throughout this book I have mentioned some basic first aid related to some of the temperatures and conditions that you may find yourself hiking through. I just want to mention here that if your dog does injure itself to where heading back is impossible or life threatening, tie him up to a spot that not only provides shelter, but to a spot that can be found again. Mark your map, know where you are and how to tell a rescuer to get there. Build a siting marker that can be seen from the sky, and one that can be seen from a ground approach as well. If it is going to be cold, make sure and put his poncho on him. Make sure and leave lots of water, and food if it does not further the injury. Clean and cover any open wound. Treat the condition as best you can, leave a note explaining the situation should anyone else come along, and get to help.

If you think you may be able to get him out, a litter can be made from a pack frame, or tent poles and your foam pad. Splints can be made from your tent poles or sticks along with the foam pad as well.

Not to sound trite, but prevention is the best medicine. Not many people understand first aid, CPR for people or dogs, or have much training in it. Though this is not a book on first aid, it goes hand in hand with going out in the wilderness. I always carry a first aid book for people, with a quick reference section, so if there was a situation, I could immediately look up what to do, rather than guess and possibly cause further damage.

So far, to my knowledge that type of book for dogs does not exist. It is my belief that it should be a book separate from a training book, so that it would be small, and easily transported in either your pack or your dogs.

If this is something that you are interested in, feel free to write me at Insight Out Publications, 3243 Arlington Ave. Box 137, Riverside, CA 92506 or E-Mail me at insightout@earthlink.net and I will try to keep you informed on the decision and progress of this undertaking.

In the meanwhile, it's always wise to discuss with your vet the best preventative measures to take in your area, or where you plan on hiking. Make sure you know where the nearest vet is from the area you plan on going to. And try and use the same common sense approach to your dogs health and well being as you would for a child.

Happy Trails

CHAPTER XII

Poisonous Plants

Here is a short list of plants to avoid. Obviously there may be more throughout the country, but most people are hard pressed to identify all of these. The more knowledge-able you are of the area you are hiking the safer it will be for both you and your dog. Often times the local ranger station will have brochures to hand out or at least pictures on the wall of possible dangerous plants, animals and insects. Study the pamphlets and brochures that are available to you in your state and always keep a lookout for some of these potential dangers. Some dogs are naturally quite smart at avoiding some poisonous things, but they do not know all the different plants and it is your job to be aware of them.

I suggest a trip in your area, where you specifically go out and try to identify plants or other potential dangers before bringing your pooch out with you.

Many of these plants are house plants. Some dogs will eat anything when they are hungry and left alone. Make sure and identify the plants in and around your house. Best not to let him eat anything off the ground.

Common House Plants

Caladium

Castor bean

Christmas rose

Dieffenbachia

Dumb cane

Elephant's ear

Jerusalem cherry

Mistletoe

Philodendron

Poinsettia

Rosary pea

Trees and Shrubs (Leaves, Berries, Bark)

Apricot

Avocado

Azalea

Black locust

Boxwood

Chinaberry

Horse chestnut

Holly

Oak

Oleander

Privet

Rhododendron

Wild black cherry

Yew

Ornamental Plants

Daphne

English Ivy

Gold chain

Lantana

Mountain laurel

Yellow jessamine

Wisteria

Field and Woods Plants

Buttercup

Black-eyed Susan

Coneflower

Deadly nightshade

Foxtail

Goldenglow

Hemlock

Jack-in-the-pulpit

Jimsonweed

Mushrooms

Nightshade

Nettle

Pokeweed

Sandbur

Vegetables and Leaves

Tomato

Potato

Rhubarb

Garden Flowers

Autumn crocus

Bleeding heart

Daffodil

Foxglove

Jonquil

Larkspur

Lily of the valley

Monkshood

Narcissus

APPENDIX

Since the release of this book, (formerly titled "Happy Trails For You and Your Dog") I received a great deal of feedback. Internet dog-hike-list discussions and seminars for local dog-hike clubs have yeilded a variety of interesting and varied opinions from people all over the country. This appendix addresses the most frequently asked questions, (F.A.Q.) and other problems you may be having.

Always check with your vet to see if there are additional factors involved in your dog's breed, age or health. Veterenarians have their differences also, though one would hope that there would be less speculation and more fact when it came to medical matters.

Here are the most debated and asked about topics. Your opinions and experiences are welcome. They can be sent to me through ICS Books.

G.H.

F.A.Q.

Where can I hike with my dog?

Obviously I can not cover every area of the world or the U.S. within the confines of this book. It would be best to look up the phone numbers of your local Forest Service, National Parks, Bureau of Land Management, and State Parks, and ask them for the most current information. It changes constantly.

Be sure to ask not only if it is legal to hike with your dog, find out specific leash laws, where you can camp, and if there have been any problems with the spreading of diseases or other hazards specific to the area.

Does my dog need to be on a leash?

This is a heavily debated topic. In a perfect world the answer would be a simple no, he doesn't have to be.

First of all, there are leash laws in many areas so you need to check where you are going and call to find out if there are any regulations. Some parks even have requirements on the length of the leash.

On one hand we have the freedom people who believe we have the right to do whatever we want, in so much as we are not committing actual crimes. And also on the side of the "no leash people" we have the "dogs are animals, and animals are wild" theory. Lastly, in defense of the no leash argument, it is a pleasant experience to hike with a well trained dog through the countryside, and most certainly off leash would be the dogs preference. Now the key word here is, "well trained", which too often owners translate to "doesn't bite, and doesn't run away". Just because you know that your dog doesn't bite, doesn't mean the approaching family knows that. Most people find it a frightening experience to be approached by loose dogs, and that is ruining someone else's peace.

In any case, this isn't a perfect world, and you might ask yourself if you trust everyones judgment when you answer this question for yourself. Dogs seem to take a liking or disliking to some people for no apparent reason. There are many dogs just dying to take a chunk out of the next dog they see, and if you are like most loyal dog owners, you truly love your dog and don't view this as a funny thing, or may the best dog win. It seems to be macho man, with macho dog that is out to prove how tough his dog is.

I have had my fill of encounters with loose dogs, and I know this is the prime reason for the banning of dogs in many areas. Loose dogs frighten people, crap in places we don't know so it doesn't always get cleaned up, and most of them seem to be the ones who want to eat my dogs. Loose dogs chase wildlife, that have all they can do to survive from day to day without expending more energy just to be driven away from their tasks by someones "freedom dog".

On another note, if you have read the section about dogs drinking tainted water, than you can see how it would be impossible to stop them from drinking out of streams and lakes if they were not on a lead. I also just was told of a dog that ended up in a coyote trap. This also would not happen if the dog had been leashed. Along the way I will cite other valid reasons for keeping your dog leashed at all times.

What do I do if my dog does get in a fight?

Few people liked my theory on pulling on the losing dog. I admit it is not a tactic I am terribly fond of, but a trainer I know insists that it has its place.

After much heated discussion, it seems that pepper spray/mace is the winner, though it does have its drawbacks. On a windy day you could end up spraying yourself, and there is always the possibility that it may not work. All in all, short of a gun, it is the best defense.

There are several formulas of sprays on the market, but I have no information on which one is most effective. I would like to add to be sure and find the owner of the attacking dog and spray them as well, just for good measure. After all, they are to blame—not the dog.

What if my dog is bitten by a snake?

I would like to share the information I have gathered recently. If it all seems confusing, it's because it is. Read the information, update yourself as best you can with the colleges or vets you respect, and make the best decision you can.

The vet I spoke to in the mountains here in California deals with snake bites more often than many other vets. Most vets in cities don't even carry the expensive anti-venom. He is not a believer of using snake-bite kits. He doesn't feel that they are affective, and says people can end up causing more damage than if they would have left the wound alone. Now my purpose in this book, is not to give, "take the dog to a vet" answers, but unless you are wealthy and knowledgeable enough to carry and use anti-venom, you may decide for yourself to try and use a snake bite kit. The "Extractor" is the most popular kit on the market today, and is available in most sporting goods stores.

Some veteranarians are using an injectable steroid as an anti-inflamatory to stop the tissue destruction that occurs from snake bites. The drug is packaged in a two part vial, that is temperature and time stable. As of this writing I can not find more information on this treatment. Contact your vet, or a veteranary college to see what progress has been made.

The use of a tourniquet is arguable. I would not use one unless you are many miles in, and have emergency training and know exactly what to look for when a tourniquet has been applied. Tourniquets are placed just above the wound, to stop the flow of blood to the heart. (Often times snakes bite dogs on the nose, and obviously a tourniquet can not be used in this situation.) Applying ice to the inflicted area will slow down the spread of venom as well.

If you did your research before beginning your hike, you will know where the local vet is located, and have his phone number with you, or in your car. The sad truth is that unless your dog is a certified search and rescue dog, (SAR) no-one will med-flight him out of the wilderness.

In my research involving snake bites, many people have commented on the effectiveness of snake training for dogs. This is where snakes have had their venom producing glands removed and dogs are trained to fear snakes.

From what I have gathered, all the cards are not in on the total effectiveness of this type of training. Some dogs just don't get it, or forget it. The worst thing that can happen is having a false sense of security. My personal opinion is, if you are interested in training of this type and can afford it, go for it. Just keep in mind that there is no guarantee, and you should be as careful and aware had the training never occurred. If the dog has learned . . . great! If not, then you will have at least made an effort to be as safe and careful as possible.

Many dogs have been bitten by poisonious snakes and have survived. As a matter of fact, they usually do. A very knowledgeable friend of mine, Jim Greenway, suggests that evolution has played a great part in the survival of dogs being bitten by snakes. He says selective pressure has weeded out many dogs that were vulnerable to envenomation.

Jim also suggests that fear and perception may be the key. When a dog is bitten by a snake, he doesn't know enough to realize he could die or be very sick. It just hurts. Without that fear, the heart rate and blood pressure do not send the venom skyrocketing through the circulatory system. Jim asks, "are dogs to dumb to die?"

It's a tough one to call. Evaluate your situation and make a calm decision. If you are a long way out with a large dog, or any dog for that matter, the best solution may be to hang out where you are. Keep calm, set up your camp, and keep your dog as quiet and relaxed as possible. Wait it out and see how it goes. Often times snakes do not inject venom in their bites at all. Babies are the worst. They are dumb and inject all of their venom in a bite, where as adult snakes may bite to defend themselves and only inject venom when they want to kill for a meal.

One more reason for keeping your dog on a leash.

Can I get more information on protecting my dogs feet?

There are many dog booties on the market these days. Summer and Winter protection, booties are made from strong Cordura material, and from Polar Tec, and Neoprene, and combinations of materials.

Booties help keep ice balls from forming between toes, and give feet a wider base on the snow. They also help prevent abrasion from ice, or granite or any rough or hot surface.

Some of the new dog booties stay up better than some of the older designs, but it is common practice to hold them up with either duct tape or vet wrap which doesn't stick to the fur like tapes. They only need be wrapped tight enough to hold, not so they are restricting.

There are also some products on the market to help toughen up and protect pads such as Mushers Secret, which claims to prevent salt damage, snow ball build-up and other things. There is Pad Kote by Happy Jack. It is a blue liquid that claims to aid in healing and toughening. Also Protecta-Pad, by Tomlyn which says it is for dry and cracking pads of working and hunting dogs. As mentioned in the book, soaking dogs pads in tannic acid made from a strong Lipton type tea seams to be a tried and true method.

Here are a couple other "home made" recipes to help dogs pads, shared by Linda von Hanneken-Martin of Wolf Packs.

Treatment:

        2-3 lbs of Vaseline

        75cc's of Betadine

        1 lb of Lanolin

        1/2 lb of glycerin

        40 cc's of DMSO

Booties:

Dog booties can be made at home from old fat tire inner tubes. Of course you need to find the proper diameter. The top is then duct taped or vet wrapped to the dogs leg, the toe end left open to shed stones and water. If you can use a sewing machine, all the materials necessary for most booties are available from fabric stores.

My advice is to buy quality products and leave the sewing to the experts.

Is there anything that can truly remove skunk odor?

You would think that in this high-tech world of life-saving drugs and formulas to re-grow hair, that a simple matter of finding an efficient way of de-oderizing your pet after a skunk encounter would be easy enough.

Well, good news—its here. And its been here for a few years. The reason you may not of heard of it, is because its not for sale. No, that's not the bad news. The reason its not for sale, is that if it were to be bottled, it would explode. It's a simple formula you can make at home since most people already have the ingredients in their house.

Simply mix one quart of off-the-shelf 3% hydrogen peroxide, 1/4 cup of baking soda, and a teaspoon of liquid soap, such as dish soap, not laundry soap. Bathe your pet in the solution being careful not to get any in the eyes, nose or mouth. Wait about five to ten minutes and rinse thoroughly with ordinary tap water. That's it! And no, you will not have a bleached blonde pet. You certainly won't have a tomato red dog.

Here is how this wonderful formula came to be:

Paul Krebaum, a chemist at Molex Inc. in Lisle Illinois, was looking for a way to neutralize the sulphur smell of a gas given off by chemical reactions in his lab. He reasoned that it would be better to destroy the gas rather than to vent it into the atmosphere.

Krebaum had extensive experience with "thiols"— chemicals that impart a stench to skunk spray, decaying fecal matter, and decomposing flesh. He surmised that hydrogen peroxide would neutralize thiols by inducing them to combine with oxygen.

Later when a friends cat was sprayed by a skunk, Krebaum deduced that skunk spray was made up of thiols, and suggested using a variation of the formula he used in the lab. The next day his friend said the stuff worked like magic, and that every trace of skunk odor was completely gone from the cat.

Being a scientist, Krebaum needed proof of his own. While driving down the highway on a cold February day, he noticed (probably smelled) a skunk that had been killed on the road, and was quite pre-served from the freezing temperature. He carefully wrapped the skunk inside two plastic bags and put it in the trunk of his car.

As he made up the solution behind his office, his eyes were watering the entire time. He dunked the skunk in a bucket of his formula, and immediately the smell went away.

Krebaum had considered trying to figure out a way to patent his formula, but quickly abandoned the idea. Once the hydrogen peroxide is mixed with the baking soda it is no longer stable. It can not be stored in a bottle or it would explode. He decided instead to make it a free gift to humanity.

Thank you Mr. Krebaum.

Can you clear up the causes of a condition called bloat?

Bloat, actually called gastric torsion, or gastric dilation-volvulus syndrome (GDV) is one of the more serious conditions that can affect any dog. Dilation of the stomach, (bloating) combined with twisting or displacement of the stomach from its normal position is life threatening because the stomach can not be emptied.

GDV is most common in large, deep chested dogs, though it can occur in any breed. The contributing factor is the way an animal is fed in conjunction with exercise. Dogs that are fed exclusively dry dog food are at a higher risk than dogs fed canned, or a mixture of canned and dry food, the reason being that dry dog food tends to expand in the stomach when it absorbs fluid.

It is thought that adding water to dry dog food will lessen the possibility of bloat, better yet would be to add a small amount of canned food to the dry with warm water for a gravy affect.

Most important is the timing of meals relative to exercise. Meals should be withheld for at least one hour after vigorous exercise to allow a dogs' body to cool down. After meals it is also advisable to wait an hour before any vigorous activity is resumed. If this does not conform to your days activities, meals can either be withheld until the end of the day, or small amounts of food can be given throughout the day. It is important to keep in mind that maintaining your usual feeding schedule is best , and do not change the brand of food your pet is used to.

Clinical signs associated with GDV are: excessive salivation, abdominal distension, restlessness, nonproductive vomiting, rapid, shallow breathing and pale gums.

Dogs most at risk are: German Shepards, Irish Setters, Standard Poodles, Great Danes, and Doberman Pinschers.

What if my dog eats a poisonous plant?

Keep in mind we are talking about plants, and not other types of poisoning. There are different remedies for different kinds of poisoning. I have listed the most poisonous plants in the book, but it is safe to assume that all house plants are poisonous, and a great deal of plants found outside. It is also a possibility that plants could have been sprayed with toxic chemicals as well. Another good reason to keep your dog on a leash.

People often use salt as a product to induce vomiting. It can work, and in a pinch, (forgive the pun) given in the proper amount, salt can induce vomiting. The problem is 1/2 teaspoon per pound of dog weight can be fatal.

One teaspoon of 3% hydrogen peroxide per ten

pounds of body weight every ten minutes is the method recommended by some vets. Adding syrup of ipecac to your first aid kit is the best remedy, and should be something that is kept in every house as well. The formula for syrup of ipecac is one teaspoon for every ten pounds of your dogs weight. It takes a while longer to work on dogs than it does on humans, so you should wait a while. It can be repeated if there are no results.

A couple of methods of giving dogs these medicines are to drip the solution into the corner of the dogs mouth, while holding his head up. You can pull back the bottom lip and trickle it in. Another is to apply a mouth tie loosely to limit jaw movement, tip the dogs head slightly back and then make a pouch out of the lower lip. Allow each small amount to be swallowed before giving any more of the dose.

If salt is all you have, grasp the upper jaw with one hand over the muzzle, press the lips over the upper teeth by pressing your thumb on one side and your fingers on the other so the dogs' lips are between its teeth and your fingers. Firm pressure will force his mouth open. Holding the teaspoon of salt in the other hand, place the salt as far back in the mouth as possible, close and gently rub the throat to stimulate swallowing. The formula for salt is a heaping teaspoon every ten minutes till the dog vomits.

How about a quick reference on dog C.P.R.

C.P.R. or Cardiopulmonary Resuscitation, should be given when the dog is not breathing, and has no heartbeat. (To check for a heartbeat, feel behind the chest behind the left elbow). *Figure A.*

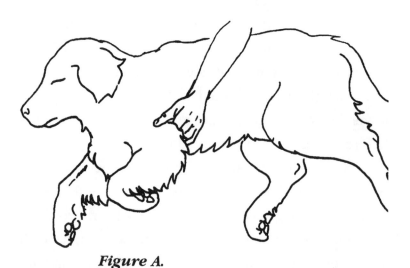

Figure A.

Check the dogs mouth or nose for any foreign substance that may be blocking his airway. For a small dog, you can hold him upside down by the hind legs and shake. For a large dog, lay him on his side, and if necessary use a long nose pliers to remove any obstruction.

Figure B.

IF THERE IS A HEARTBEAT

To perform mouth to nose resuscitation, lay the dog on his right side. Close his mouth and place your mouth over the dogs nose and blow into it five or six times. **Figure B.** (For puppies, breaths are short and shallow, for big dogs, breaths are long and deep). If breathing is not restored, apply resuscitation at the rate of one breath every three seconds.

IF THERE IS NO HEARTBEAT

Push with the heel of your hand between the third and sixth ribs, ***Figure C.*** just below the left elbow. Force used varies with the size of the dog. Give ten quick compression's and check for a heartbeat. If there still is no heartbeat, continue cardiac compression at the rate of ten compression's every six seconds.

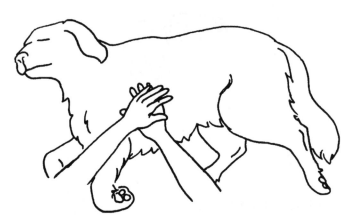

Figure C.

IF BREATHING AND HEARTBEAT HAVE STOPPED

Give ten cardiac compression's followed by two mouth to nose breaths. Repeat at the rate of ten cycles per minute, or one sequence every ten seconds.

If after ten minutes there is still no sign of heartbeat and pulse, and the gums and tongue are blue, the pupils are dilated and there is no reaction when the surface of the eye is touched, you can presume the dog is dead.

My goal is not to scare anyone, but to make people aware of potential problems before they occur, and on the rare occasion when there is a situation, to be prepared. When it comes to first aid, there are dozens of other incidents that may occur. My recommendation is to take an EMT course, or any training for first aid and CPR that may be offered in your area. Always carry a first aid book for people and one for dogs. Find a book that's easy to read, and familiarize yourself with it before tucking it away in your pack. You may not remember every procedure, but at least you will know where the book is, and where you can find the information needed. Panic is your worst enemy. Better to take the time to apply first aid correctly, rather than a frenzied guess.

I can tell you that there are rarely any problems on the hikes I have taken in many years. With knowledge of what to do in a problem situation comes confidence and peace. Avoiding potential danger is the key to a successful adventure.

May all of your hiking experiencs be trouble free and filled with joy.

Gary Hoffman

INDEX